There's a Man

A Psychic Medium's S

Cop

Writte

Chapter 1- The Shift

It was 1987, and I was living in Sarasota, Florida with my roommate Sally. She told me some of her friends visited a local psychic and I should go to see this psychic. Sally thought that the psychic would help me for whatever reason I did not know. I decided to call this psychic since I was more curious than anything. I had been to another psychic when I was a teen a few years before with my mother and I felt that I benefited from the experience but I thought that psychic was little strange with her crystal ball but her prediction that I would be working to help others on a spiritual level seemed off at the time since I was planning then on pursuing a music therapy degree.

Much had changed from my teen years to this time when I was twenty-eight years old. I thought I was managing quite well despite the past traumas that had occurred with me over the past ten years but for some reason my roommate, Sally, thought differently. Little did she know she was helping me on my journey to be a psychic medium which I did not know I would pursue as a future profession.

I made an appointment with this local psychic whose name was Mary. She asked me to bring to the appointment some piece of jewelry or hand-held item from a passed loved one I wanted to connect. She said this would help her connect with the persons I wanted to discuss in the reading. This was something new to me since my idea of having a reading was with cards or nothing at all. I decided to bring my deceased father's wristwatch that he wore daily since he was one of my family members I had questions about.

It had been ten years since the disappearance of my father and brother. My life had significant changes since that time in my life and the lives of my other living family members. The changes were so extreme that it felt like someone snatched me up and threw me into a whole new planet with people who looked the same as my previous life but who acted different as if they never knew me. Those people whom I trusted at the time seemed to disappear and only a couple of people remained in my life. I knew I was dramatically different from then and was in survival mode now for ten years but was functioning. Life had dramatically changed also for my other living brother and my mother as well as my other extended family. One of my cousins told me that when my father died, her living father's spirit died even though he was physically still here. We all dealt with the losses of my father and brother in radically different ways. I knew our lives would never be the same as it securely was.

Ten years later, I was cautiously seeking answers regarding their disappearance. The day soon came when I was going to see Mary, the psychic, for answers to questions I had stuffed away deeply in my unconscious since I felt I was managing the results of the trauma fine overall. I had accepted that only God would know the answers and I would have to live with the unanswered questions of how and why the accident and loss happened to our family. But there were curiosity and fear factors regarding if this psychic would have any information to these deep-rooted questions. I figured that if the psychic information did not make sense to me that would have been fine since I felt I was also psychic and it would be fun to connect with someone that may have similar psychic abilities.

This knowledge of knowing that I was very psychic since as far back in my life as I could remember was an accepted although not readily shared part of myself. I recall as a young as four years old that I would see visions and feel the presence of apparitions zooming around in places I resided and visited. I did not share this with anyone but my mother and sometimes my paternal grandmother at the time. I felt like they would think I was crazy even though they never said those words but would only give me an odd look while trying to not further discuss my psychic experiences.

Thus, after the loss of my brother and father, I had very vivid dreams and visitations from them and other deceased family members. Since my grief and loss was more than anything I had ever experienced, I questioned if what I was seeing was real or just my wishes and dreams to keep them alive in my head. I was hoping Mary, the psychic medium, would help to clarify this conflict for me. I went to the reading with an open mind but honestly, I was not optimistic about what I would hear.

Arriving at Mary's house, I parked my car in a circular gravel driveway and entered her home with a sign that read "Come In." Inside the door was another sign that said, "Please remove your shoes." I did as the sign instructed but wondered if I am going to be on a scavenger hunt to see Mary. I started having my doubts as I sat on the outdated upholstered yellow couch that was placed on this very odd colored emerald green carpet. As I sat patiently waiting, I heard people talking in the next room who I assumed one of them was Mary. Their session sounded like it was ending. The person who just completed her reading left through the emerald green carpeted room with a look of contentment and no tears. I started feeling a little better and optimistic at this point. Mary then appeared in the doorway and invited me in with a warm welcome and smile.

Mary had crystal blue eyes with grey hair that was styled high on her head. She appeared to be in her 70's and was dressed very comfortably but stylish; not like the stereotypical gypsy looking psychics with crystal balls I saw on TV. I followed her to her reading room with an oversized boom box where Mary recorded the readings on cassette tapes. I started to feel more comfortable and felt like I knew this woman from somewhere but could put my finger on where. We sat next to each other, her in her chair and I on another odd upholstered couch with the same color carpet as the waiting room. She proceeded to explained how she did readings then as she more closely looked into my eyes said that she was also here to give me tips on how to do psychic readings. I looked at her with a puzzled look since I was there for a reading not a lesson. She was insistent that I listen to her. She proceeded to tell me within a matter of minutes that I also was very psychic and will be helping a lot of people in the future deal with grief as a medium someday. I just smiled and looked at her with caution and doubt since I thought maybe she tells everyone this. I told her I wanted to connect with my father and brother who passed ten years ago but she continued to instruct me in how to be a medium. I listened and thought, well that's nice but what about my father and brother. She told me she was assigned to motivate me to do readings for others and the information was given to her from my guides and angel beings. She said I am very blessed and gifted. Mary said she felt like I was like a granddaughter to her. I also felt an instant connection. She instructed me in protection techniques and trusting what I see and hear which seemed foreign to me but somewhat beneficial and interesting. Mary then proceeded to connect with my deceased grandmother, whose name was also Mary, who told her to thank me for the red rose. No one knew I had placed one red rose on my grandmother's coffin following the funeral. She continued to describe my grandmother's physical and personality characteristics and how my grandmother protects me as the gate keeper to who can connect with me on the other side. While she was alive, she was someone whom I trusted and felt like we had a special bond from the time I was very small. We had spent a lot of treasured time together when she was alive, and I missed her dearly. I realized then that this psychic was truly connecting with information from my grandmother who had gone to the other side a few years prior.

My father's wristwatch was in my pocket. I pulled it out and gave it to Mary who proceeded to tell me more than I asked for regarding my father's background and about his likes and dislikes; some of them I knew and some I questioned. I then needed to know the big questions, how did he die and why was he and my brother missing for a year after they were considered dead or missing. She saw him with two others in cold water with guns. I told her they had supposedly drowned while they were duck hunting which included my brother another man and his son. She said their passing was very quick and they did not suffer for more than a few minutes. It was painful to hear but somewhat answered my questions.

She then told me my father did not know he had passed and was roaming around trying to talk to my mother, other brother and I but was very frustrated since we were not responding to this presence. She said his father, my grandfather, who had passed when I was twelve, then came to my father and told him he had died. At that time, he could cross over with my brother to the other side. She said the perception of time was very different on the other side and it may have been years, according to our earthly time, that my father realized he was really gone physically from this earthly world. That made sense to me since I did not have any dreams or visions of them until about three years following their disappearance but only felt a dark and disconnected emptiness.

The reading with Mary lasted close to two hours and I received more information than I asked for. This reading was more psychologically helpful than the years of psychotherapy and hypnosis I received following the accident; not to discredit the therapy which helped somewhat with how to cope with this extreme and disruptive loss. The reading gave me a sense of peace and hope that I had not felt in close to a decade.

Following the reading, I called my mother who lived in Ohio at the time and told her the oddities and interesting information Mary had said regarding my father and grandmother. My mother positively confirmed everything the reading revealed even the odd statement that I questioned when he would ask my mom to put in oysters in the Thanksgiving dressing as a tease every year but she refused. I never knew they had that conversation. My father had a unique way of adding flair and curiosity to others lives with his funny statements. I listened to the cassette tape recording of this reading more times than I can remember and was astounded how a woman who never met me told me a treasure of secrets and very healing information about the past and passing of those I missed every day of my life. I wondered if she was accurate about me doing readings for others in the future though. At the time, I did not take it seriously but kept the idea on the back burner for a future but unlikely possibility, I thought.

Fast forward twenty-seven years from that time, I now live in Arizona, have two children, and am standing in classroom of college students at a local university talking my psychic life. I followed Mary's advice and prediction to professionally practice my work as a psychic medium as well as a speaker and author; quite a shift from my thoughts of my future in 1987. I guess Mary was accurate after all, despite the fact I was in denial and hid my medium psychic skills from just about everyone but my mother. Looking back now, I am incredibly grateful I had the few sessions with Mary, the psychic, as I consider her one of my most influential mentors.

Now I was telling my story to these young college students who to my surprise were interested in listening and asking me questions about how I became a psychic medium. This was the moment I decided to write this memoir and book in hopes to inspire others and just entertain a few. Standing at the front of the classroom at this university, I proceeded to tell my story starting when I was only four years old. I realized then that my thoughts, visions, and dreams were not like the average little girl. I told them that many a night as a child, I would lie at night in my bedroom trying to sleep but instead was consumed with anxiety and fear. My bedroom was removed from the rest of the family on the first floor while they all slept on the second floor. When I screamed in fear in the middle of the night usually, I was seeing things or hearing things but no one in the house initially heard me. I felt so isolated and petrified to sleep in my room alone, but I continued to do so since it was my room. Sometimes I was so scared that no sound would come out of my mouth when trying to scream for help as I lay on my bed with my covers over my head. This would happen especially during the nights when I would visualize spirit forms coming out of my bedroom wall and moving towards me. Some nights, my poor pregnant mother would come all the way down the stairs from her second-floor bedroom and try to calm me in her exhausted and frustrated manner while telling me that nothing is down here. But I knew better, I saw apparitions and faces outside in the window and in my room trying to scare me. I heard my name called often and I sensed with my eyes closed that some kind of being or spirit was there. These fearful nights went on for close to a year when my parents decided it was fine for me to sleep with my younger brother, Charlie, in his twin bed upstairs where the rest of the family slept. I still felt fearful presences but for some reason having Charlie there helped me to sleep and not scream in terror at night. Also, being closer to my parents decreased my anxiety but the spirts, images and voices were still there. I did not know how to stop them. Often when the nighttime interferences became too overwhelming, I would walk to my parent's room and I tell them I was scared. My mother used to tell me once again there was nothing there and I have nothing to fear.

Years later, my mother apologized for getting frustrated and not being honest with me during those childhood nights of terror and confusion. She told me then that she also saw visions outside my bedroom window and felt the apparitions in that house. I wished she would have told me back then how she felt the same things. It may have helped me not grow up thinking I was losing my mind.

When we moved out of that house three years later, I continued to sense spirit presence. Despite that, I felt I could sleep better with my brothers and parents in the next bedrooms. I realized then that I was not crazy just sort of psychic but not sure where this ability would take me if anywhere. I also developed from my school influence the connection with prayer which helped me to sleep.

Chapter 2- Growing Up

Growing up from a young child to teen, I would experience weekly incidents of sleep disturbances, weird and fearful dreams, and visions of apparitions. My best way to describe these apparitions is they are fast moving shadows to detailed images of people rapidly moving through our world. Some are white, grey and some are black while some have very clear clothing and facial features but they move very fast and are usually two to three feet from the ground.

One vivid apparitional memory was when I was in third grade spending the night at a friend's house which was over fifty years old and being renovated. During the middle of the night, I had to go to the bathroom. Prior to walking into the bathroom, I heard water running in the bathtub. Upon approaching the bathroom door, I then saw an older grey-haired woman in spirit who appeared to be dead floating in the bathtub. Well, I did not go into that bathroom again or did I ever spend the night there. It was a frightful sight that I vividly recall to this day. I asked my friend who lived there if an old lady lived in her house before they did, and she told me yes there was, and she died in the bathroom. That was enough information for me to stay clear of that house and know, yes again, I had the ability to see those who had passed. I never told anyone until years later about this incident. To this day when I drive by that house, I see the bathroom scene once again.

The school I attended was a Catholic elementary school which helped me to learn the peace, protection, and benefits of prayer. I learned the prayers of the rosary and to this day continue to do the rosary to help me sleep when I feel like I am being disturbed by spirit energy. But there were many rules and regulations that I never understood. We were required to attend daily morning mass, which was quite early and regimented, but it helped me to develop self-discipline even though I vehemently rebelled from some of the rules. For instance, we had to wear a veil or hat on our head during mass. I thought it was ridiculous that God would make us cover our head to pray. I decided one day that I would put a Kleenex on my head and attach it with bobby pins instead of the veil or the beanie that had us wear. To this day, I recall one of the nuns, who I knew did not appreciate my rebellious nature, staring at me as I walked into the mass and sat down with my idea of a head cover for mass. I was reprimanded by that nun after the mass to wear the proper attire during the next mass which I randomly adhered to. Many mornings, I intentionally did not have my head covered. Another example, involving mandatory clothing, was that we were to wear our skirts at knee level or below. I again thought this was a stupid rule and challenged the skirt rule by intentionally rolling up my skirt while at lunch and on the playground. Some of my friends did the same rebellious act. The nuns decided to have an all-girl educational session about how short skirts were the influence of the devil. I recall leaving that session with more thoughts of rebellion and wondering why God would care about the length of our skirts. This was the 1960's and the world was changing with the fashion of miniskirts and shorts with boots which of course I wore when not at school. Despite all that rebellion, I did rely on that Catholic influence and education for the religious faith and trust that I still hold to this day that has helped me with my fear of psychic experiences. I rely on my silent prayers for protection and guidance when doing readings which I believe influences the quality of the readings I perform. But I believe in this world of social misconception about psychics, this rebellious nature helped me to have the courage to do what I felt God wanted me to do as a medium. I don't think that personality characteristic is something that will disappear. I believe it has benefited me through all the lifetime challenges I have dealt with.

Chapter 3 - More Early Premonitions and Visitations

Throughout my teen years, it seemed my abilities for seeing the future were occurring more often with accuracy. I recall telling everyone in my family that my paternal grandpa is not coming home from his surgery and that he was going to die. No one believed me as they said his surgery is simple and he would be home in a few days. I recall crying hysterically with the knowing that I would never see him again. Following his surgery, he did not come home, and he passed within the week. I was close to my grandfather and had difficulty coping with his loss. It was a devastating loss for me and many others in the family. He was the patriarch of our family, well respected in the community, and the president of our family's steel foundry. Life was not the same after he passed for me. This was my first experience of losing someone close to me. I started to become more depressed, introverted and did not express my emotions very well to anyone including my family. It was like the lights went out in my world.

Another psychic event happened that was very memorable and disturbing when I was sixteen. I experienced fear beyond my understanding and an out of body experience. I know I was not dreaming. It was about 4:00 in the morning and my brothers and parents were sleeping. My brothers slept on the first-floor bedroom and my parents on the third floor. Once again, my bedroom was isolated from the rest of the family. My bedroom was on the second floor where the main entrance was located. As I was waking up, I felt breathing and someone lying on my side facing me as I was lying on my left side. At first, I thought it was one of my brothers since one of them had a history of sleep walking or maybe they were playing a practical joke on me. But when I opened my eyes, I saw a young man with medium frame with dark hair and eyes staring at me. My next thought was that maybe my boyfriend had somehow snuck into the house and was playing a funny joke on me. Within seconds I realized it was not either of my brothers nor my boyfriend but a stranger who felt all too familiar but with some ambiguity. Then the young man said to me in a calm and quiet manner, "Don't worry, I won't hurt you." At that point, I could not breathe or scream as I closed my eyes and was filled with overwhelming fear. Instantly, I was looking down at myself in the bed with this dark-haired young man next to me with a sensation of peace and contentment. I was not in my body anymore as I floated in the upper corner of my room looking down at my body. It felt elating and free but within the minute I was back in my body and the young man was gone. I took a sigh of relief that he was gone as my heart was rapidly beating and I sat up in bed not knowing what to think. I knew at this point this was not a human but a spirit coming to visit me for some reason of which to this day I have no idea why he visited me. He did not have angel wings or a smile just a strong presence. My out of body experience is one of the most vivid and memorable experiences I have had to this day. Years later, I had another similar out of body experience but this time I was terribly ill with a raging temperature. I survived that one too. Both times, I realized, if this was what it was like to die then I will have no fear but fearless anticipation to leave my body once again whenever God wants me. I told my mother about these experiences, but she had no comment and looked at me as if I was crazy, I thought. But there was more to her story as to why she reacted in this manner.

A few days after my psychic visitation, a psychic woman whom my mother knew called my mother and stated she saw me in a vision in distress. The psychic, whom I do not recall her name, said that an item in our house in the northwest side of the home was attracting spirits that are disturbing your daughter when she sleeps. I continued to not sleep well after that night, getting up numerous times in the night and saying many prayers to help me try to sleep. My mother looked in the side of the home the psychic described, and she found an Ouija board. A week later, I felt like my fear of sleeping had somehow released and I felt peace instead of fear at night. My mother then informed me she destroyed and removed the board from the home. She did not tell me immediately about the board but asked me if I was sleeping better. It was at that point then she informed me of the call from the psychic and removing the board. I was thankful that the psychic relied that information to my mother or I know I would have repeated my multiple fearful restless nights like I did when I was younger.

But the question remained, was the young man who appeared to me a spirit attracted from the board or was he one of my spirit guides. Now I think that he was a spiritual visitor just trying to connect to someone, sort of a lost soul.

My mother was also psychic thus she understood my abilities and sensitivities. I felt she was the only person I could share my thoughts and feelings with but I continued to hide my psychic gifts from the rest of the world for fear they would judge me and reject me. She told me to keep the psychic information at home and only with her and my aunt, her sister. I wanted to be popular as most teens do but I thought this information would not improve my popularity with my friends at school.

Throughout the next year, I became very depressed to the point that I could not think clearly or interact with the world without extreme anxiety. I was not sure if all the negativity was removed from the house or I was just becoming more receptive to connecting with spirit and other's emotions. My parents decided to bring me to a psychologist and psychiatrist who prescribed anti-anxiety medication and psychotherapy.

When I had the medication in my system, I did not feel much of anything especially spirit information, but I was still depressed and once again having difficulty sleeping. They performed multiple personality and psychological tests with the conclusion that I was in the gifted IQ category but had an anxiety disorder with hypnagogic sleeping pattern disorder. They also prescribed psychotherapy to help to ease the depression. I recall during one of my psychotherapy sessions, the psychologist hypnotized me to help me to sleep. When he brought me out of hypnosis, he said to me, "You really are psychic." I thought his response was very odd coming from a psychologist and I gave him a look saying you are not telling me anything I do not know. His comment was not a surprise to me, and I am not sure what happened during that short hypnosis time, but something occurred to convince him of my psychic abilities. The hypnosis experience was very therapeutic for helping me sleep for many years following though, but I just wish I knew what information came through during the session.

Within the next year, I became more relaxed and surer of myself. I was more engaged in my interests of gymnastics, dance and playing the piano. I also was composing music that I performed throughout the community. Life was going well for me at this time, so I decided to go off the anti-anxiety medication. At that time, the spirit communication, empathic ability to feel other's feelings around me, and premonitions were once again heightened in full force. My anxiety returned but this was something I had to learn to deal with because I did not want to rely on medication for the rest of my life to function. The question was what I was to do with these abilities and how long would I be able hide them. I graduated high school then more answers came to me as my college and young adult years progressed. During that time of emerging adulthood, I traveled a journey of total transformation, extreme loss, and darkness which inspired me to help others with my therapy and intuitive psychic abilities.

Chapter 4 -The Transformation

Most people think when they go away to college that they have a liberated sense of freedom and more time to focus on themselves. My freshman year was attended at Bowling Green University in Bowling Green, Ohio while I was studying psychology and music therapy. I was quite busy with a duo major with hours of studying and involvement with music activities outside of my ordinary class work. I lived with a roommate who also was from the Akron area in a small and very compact dormitory room.

One Sunday evening in November of this freshman year, I was returning from choral practice with the Toledo Symphony Orchestra around 10:00 pm. Upon walking into my dorm room, I was looking at some other girls who lived in my dorm and my roommate sitting on the floor in my room. They told me to sit down and call my mother immediately, since it was an emergency. This was very unusual for a

Sunday night, since most of the time we were catching up on homework and preparing for the next week of classes.

I sat down as everyone was staring at me. I knew something was wrong but was not sure what. My heart started racing as I dialed my home phone number in Akron, Ohio. The look on my floor mates' faces was very distressing but I was glad they were there to support me for this obvious family emergency.

My mother answered the phone and was crying hysterically. I could hardly understand her through the hysteria. She told me my father and brother were supposed to return from their duck hunting trip in Michigan the day before. They went with another son and father duo and were staying in a cabin on a Lake Mullet near Detroit, Michigan. She told me no one had heard from them and they were considered missing. My mother could hardly contain herself, so the phone was then transferred to one of my mother's friends who told me my cousin and Aunt were on their way to pick me up. I hung up the phone as my floormates who already knew of the problem were hugging me as they told me to let them know what's going on when I get home. I was unable to speak and in a state of total shock and disbelief. My father and brother were scuba

23

divers and sailors thus were very experienced with water sports including boating and hunting for ducks which was the purpose of this trip.

My Aunt, her husband, and cousin arrived soon after. We went at now 11:00 pm to a Howard Johnson's in town for some food and coffee but I wasn't hungry. They explained to me that there was a lot going on at home and not to be alarmed. They said the newspaper and TV news would be showing the story in the next few days and there were a lot of unanswered questions. They told me that the police and Coast Guard are searching for my brother and father tomorrow. The news was beyond my comprehension of overwhelming proportions. As we drove back for the next two hours in the early morning hours now, I sat in the backseat of my Aunt's car and cried the whole entire two hour ride home back to Akron. I also prayed that God would help us understand what is going on and help to find them alive.

Upon arriving home around 2:00 am it appeared as if there was a party at our home with lots of cars and many people in the house. I managed to stop crying and act stoic for my mother who was lying on the couch in the living room and obviously was drugged on tranquilizers with lethargy. She was crying and could hardly talk to me. I immediately went into fight mode and was determined to do whatever it took to help find my missing family. I tried to sleep but was unable until a day or two later. I asked multiple questions to others in the house and contacted others involved to give me as much information as possible. I felt like I was the only one that was fighting to keep them alive and find them. It appeared no one around me had any hope they were alive except me.

When I awoke one morning after a few restless nights sleeping, I saw my paternal grandmother, Mary, and my mother both staring at me at both sides of my bed. I was barely awake and to this day felt like it was an earie dream or vision. I recall them saying to each other as I was waking up "Look at her." I have no idea what they meant while I looked at them with confusion. From that statement and their positioning on both sides of my bed I felt like I had morphed into creature or something during the night. I was speechless and then smiled at them as they both then left my bedroom. The feeling after they left has never left me since and I did morph into someone else. Someone who was very closed off from the world emotionally and someone who would not let anyone in to love me for fear they would leave and I would have to feel this God-awful pain of loss like I was feeling at that moment. Some would say that of course this traumatic loss would change or morph you. I wished it never happened, but I would not be the person I am today if I did not experience this devastating experience. The newspapers and television news had stories of the incidents as the first few weeks went on but all they found was their boat, and their belongings in the cabin but no people. I intuitively could not figure if they were alive or deceased. It was just too overwhelming for me to intuitively perceive as I continued to survive somehow in this state of shock and disbelief.

Years later, after my mother had passed, I found in my mother's memoirs of her writings of her feelings of the loss from the accident. I will say to this day it is still very painful to read. My mother wrote about the incident with following: "I am compelled to write my thoughts and feelings of the events so very tragic and painful. My husband and son left on Nov 10th,1977 for a weekend duck hunting and fishing trip in Michigan for a father and son time to have bonding with a friend and his son. I still recall their faces as I told them good-bye- smiling, excited and very happy. It was the first time in my life that I did not offer words like please be careful and do not take any chances. I expected them to return home on Saturday or Sunday. One o'clock am, two am turned into five am but still no sign of them coming home. I called the wife of the man my husband was with and she checked with neighbors in Michigan who stated they had not seen the men and the boys since the day before, Saturday when they left on the boat. They must be lost, or their boat got away with them I thought after I felt an overwhelming sense of fear and panic. The other wife chartered a plane and we with one of my husband's close friends and partners at work traveled to Michigan. Arriving finally at the cabin where the men were staying my heart was racing as I was thinking, Dear God Don't let them be dead. We can't live without them. The cabin was empty with only clothing and some other belongings scattered around but no husband or son. I was thinking, this is a nightmare. Please let me wake up and let it be over. We left the cabin without answers and totally grief stricken."

"Days go by and the boat, floatation devices and duck decoys were found but no sign of my husband and son. The coast guard and a volunteer friend who was a scuba diver were searching for days. Searching by land, air, and water but no sign of the men and their sons. They were presumed drowned and we all felt hopeless and lost. For weeks, I prayed they would walk through the door but no one was coming home. My life would never be the same and my children will never know the feeling again of a father's love and a brother's closeness. Please God help them."

My mother had written many pages of her thoughts, feelings and events following the accident, but these are one of the more poignant writings I came upon. After my mother passed in 2002, I found many more of these pages but was unable to read them until recently not because I was not interested but because reading and thinking about that time in our lives is painfully difficult despite years of therapy, hypnosis, and medium readings. I am grateful though that she did write the events and her feelings since I know it helped her and she is able to contribute to this book.

The events following the next few months are very much of a blur to me, but I recall that they called off the search for my brother and father as well as the other father son duo after three weeks; most likely since the ice was starting to form since it was a very frigid December in 1977 in Michigan. The only information we acquired was that the last people that saw them were men at the boat filling station who told the four duck hunters that a storm was a brewing and they should not go onto the lake until the storm passed. Well my father as I mentioned before was an avid sailor and scuba diver thus, I can imagine he decided he could tackle a storm if it arrived. Meanwhile, my other brother, Jay, mother, and I were left alone and hopeful that this was all a dream and they would come strolling home with ducks for us to eat and funny stories to hear about their trip. But no ducks and no stories just the emptiness of the unknown. The community, coast guard and clergy determined that most likely they were deceased thus we started the process of preparing for the end of their lives memorial ceremony without any real evidence of them passing except they were nowhere to be seen or heard of. My thoughts were thinking they had passed but I was still not wanting to believe this nor emotionally prepared to deal with this loss.

To back track the story a month or so prior, the events that lead to their missing were no coincidence but mysterious and foreboding to this day. First, my father was very well known in the area as a reputable attorney. My family had a steel foundry that my great grandfather started in the early 1900's after he immigrated here from Alsace Lorraine. One of my great uncles was the president at the time and he was planning on retiring. My father was working part time at the foundry while being groomed to be the next president of the foundry as well as continuing his current law practice. Having a history of ligation and negotiating with success, my father was negotiating with the union of the steel workers at the foundry. I recall that the union did not get all their requests for the first time in over a 50-year history of the foundry. A few weeks later, my father and brother were missing along with two others mentioned prior who also worked in a similar industry in Akron as my father. Many times, I wonder if the union's discourse somehow was a contributing factor to them missing. There is no way to know the truth at this point nearly forty years later. I hope my suspicion is incorrect, but I cannot but wonder if that discourse with the union contributed to their missing or only a coincidence. To this day we still do not know any facts that explain why they were missing except they were in a small boat and a storm was on its way. At this time in my life, I believe it was their time to go to the other side and God's will, but it took me over a decade to begin to have some level of an acceptance even without the facts or evidence of viewing them deceased. I only recall them alive and very well.

Many people have asked, since you are psychic did you have a premonition about them missing. Well yes, I did but I did not realize it until after they were missing. Months prior, my mother had decided to practice Tarot card reading. Multiple times during her reading, she would have the death card about the family. She stopped doing the cards for fear that maybe the cards would bring the bad luck or death around us. Another strange incident involved our cleaning woman who had been cleaning our house for decades. She was in the middle of cleaning one day and started screaming she found Voodoo dust in our house and that this meant death to someone in the house. She gathered her things and ran out of the house. We never saw her again from my recollection.

My premonitions were much more personable and spiritual. My brother and I were close, and we had the ability to read each other's minds as my mother used to say. One evening as I was getting ready to head back to college from being home a weekend. I was saying my Goodbye's. My brother played guitar and was a composer as I was, but I was as a pianist. He was playing a song he composed called Dawn of the Dead. I told him that the title is very morbid, and he insisted this was going to be the name of his first real song. I walked to the basement where he was playing this morbid and sort of cool rock-based song with his band. I interrupted the flow of the song to say goodbye. He only stared at me as I repeated to him, "Say Goodbye. I'm going back to school." I must have asked him five times to say bye, but he kept staring at me with a blank frozen expression that I can still see in my memory so vividly. I did not understand this behavior since he had never acted this way with me in his 15 years of growing up with me. I think he had a premonition of his passing and was not happy about it so saying goodbye was very final and not something he wanted to say. He was always funny while calling himself Ham and Cheese Man since this is what I called him, so this non-emotional blank stare was very out of his character.

My father on the other hand was outside doing his weekend yard work as I prepared to enter my car to leave. It was not unusual for him on a Sunday afternoon to be doing yard work since this was his day off from his busy law practice and foundry work. He had on his weathered and worn yellow hat and a white T-shirt which was his usual attire for yard work. My father and I were also very close, and I did not feel safe with anyone but him in my life. I had utmost respect for my father and always tried to please him by doing the right thing. I knew he loved me even though he never told me. His secure actions, attentive listening, and always being there for me spoke stronger than verbalizing any words about his feelings for me as his only daughter. Despite our close relationship, I did not as a teen ever say, "Love you Daddy" or give him a kiss on the cheek usually only a hug and a look of love. He had a goofy smile at times but was a very handsome man. But on that day I was leaving for school, he smiled that goofy smile but also did not say goodbye either, but he did say write your mother as I kissed him on the cheek. We both looked at each other in surprise. I felt like someone or a force had pushed me to give him a goodbye kiss be it an angel being or my deceased grandfather who I had dreamt about often. As I was driving off in the car away from the house, I waved goodbye then put my brakes on as I looked at my father who was now glowing with a white aura along with his goofy smile that is frozen in my memory. I had never seen this white glow aura around my father or anyone else. It took my breath away as I slowly drove off. Two weeks after that I received the phone call of their disappearance. I believe that was my premonition that he was soon to leave this world.

As mentioned earlier, we decided to prepare for their funeral type proceedings with a memorial mass with the assumption that both were deceased and not missing. That was most people's assumptions, but I was hopeful that they would be coming home and possibly were kidnapped or lost in the woods. There were hundreds of attendees at the mass where my uncles who were priests and our pastor, who was like a family member, performed the mass. I chose to sing Cat Steven's song, Morning Has Broken as a tribute to my father and brother. I understand there was not a dry eye in the congregation, but I did not notice since I was focused on singing in honor of my brother and father. I have no idea how I contrived the emotional strength to do this, but I have been known to be determined and focused in my lifetime when I want to do something. I also was in a state of shock and denial, so I believe the reality of them leaving had not hit me yet.

A month after I left school from the incidents of the accident, I returned with my schoolwork organized to complete my first semester in college. All my professors were understanding of my situation and accommodated my exams generously. Then winter break came, and I was headed back home to a solemn house and now a scant of recollection of what happened during that holiday without my beloved father and brother. I have developed amnesia presently of the decade or so that followed but throughout time others have reminded me of events during that time and I have recalled bits and pieces of the events. I have thought of getting hypnosis again to help me with this amnesia, but I feel it would not benefit me at this time in my life.

My mother meanwhile was preparing for most likely their remains to be found as she wrote from her memoirs the following: "I made arrangements for my husband and dear son's tentative burial if their bodies were found. I thought the process would be a painful experience and I was frightened. I almost copped out and called a friend to go with me to the funeral home but decided Jesus and I would go with me. When I arrived at the funeral home, I was calm and no longer filled with pain and fear. I decided that they would be buried in their hunting clothing since I believe they both would like that. We lived on earth in love with our marriage bound by God, but we are no longer earthly married but spiritually forever together." She was never the same person after that incidence and wrote in her writings how she was lonely, but she knew this was God's will and she believed she would be with them again when she passed.

My mother wrote on March 18th,1978, just 5 months after they were missing that she wrote about a dream where my father and brother were standing in front of her. She wrote: "Eliza and I had a dream this past week of my husband and her brother, beautiful Charlie. In the dream, her father told her to "Shape Up Elizabeth." She continues to write that he told her he was so sad that we were suffering but that where they are is wonderful and we should go on with our lives and we will see you in heaven. My mother then wrote, "During my dream, I felt my husband and son's arms around me. It was the closest I had felt to them since their missing. I woke up with tears and thought I must go on." Three days later, the other man's body, that was on the trip with my father, was found and within weeks so was my father's remains.

I believe it was nine months following them missing in November 1977 that one by one their remains were found in the lake. Supposedly, they were only identified by their dental records which is believable since their bodies were under water during most of the winter and some of the spring. My brave but grief-stricken mother collected some of the items my father had in his clothing of his St. Christopher medal he wore on his neck, his money clip and his Timex watch which weirdly was still ticking after being under water all that time. He also had a knife handle, but the knife blade was removed as if he was trying to cut something before he drowned. My mother gently and in her sensitive manner sat my other brother and I down in her bedroom and displayed the proof of our father being dead from the tarnished belongings. But there was nothing of evidence of my brother's since he did not have a knife or jewelry. These belongings gave me a minimal sense of closure, but I continued to look for them in public thinking they had amnesia or had to change their names for some reason. I think I was watching too many mysteries shows that stretched my imagination to this place but the closure without seeing a body or some form of illness seemed almost unattainable. Following the emerging of their bodies, we had four funerals, but I only recall two minutes of one of them and I'm not sure which one it was. I recall my previous boyfriend during high school and some college standing with his mother after the burial of one of my family members. I recall I was stoic during the service but seeing him brought me to tears since my father adored this boyfriend and so did I. I was very emotionally distraught and was unable to maintain the relationship during that time. We did get back together briefly though a few years after that while we both finished college together but that was the end of our eight-year relationship. I think God brought him into my life to be my best friend and support us during our grief, which is what he did. Like I mentioned before, I felt I could never get emotionally close to anyone again and this wore on our relationship despite the fact we still loved each other. This boyfriend was the only other person I felt completely safe with other than my father, but we moved on as I continued to deal with my grief and my journey on my own.

Another odd and uncharacteristic incident happened regarding our Christmas presents from my father. In the past prior to this incident, my father would take me out a few nights prior to the holiday to have me help him buy presents for others in the family including my mother. It was our traditional holiday shopping event that I looked forward to every year. But the year he was missing, he purchased presents for all of us prior to November which was very out of character for him. He was a last-minute shopper for all celebration events including birthdays. I think he may have had a dream or premonition of his passing. He had set up his funds for my brothers and I to have our college education taken care of and he was in process of redoing his Will. Understand my father was only 41 years old when he passed but he was an attorney with an accounting background thus he wanted us to be taken care of in the event he died but it seemed quite premature for a man in his early forties. Thus, the holiday after he was missing, we all had presents from my father which I cherish and adore even though he was not physically there to give them to us. He bought us a bible, a statue of a saint, and an owl sculpture. All unusual gifts since he would in the past buy toys, pajamas, slippers, and jewelry for us.

I thought I would have some vision, dream or clairaudient experience of my brother and father, but nothing had occurred during those months; at least as much as I remember which is not much.

Chapter 5- New Beginnings

Throughout the next few years, I continued to pursue my college degree in Occupational Therapy from Ohio State University. I had transferred from Bowling Green University to Ohio Wesleyan then completed my education at Ohio State. I did not have a lot of logical guidance since those close to me, be it friends and family, were too distraught to help me with my life goals or emotional well-being. I was on my own now where before I relied on my wise and intelligent father to guide me. The tendency to run or hide from anything remotely close to me emotionally was apparent to me and others. I think this was my way of protecting myself from feeling any more loss. My mother and other brother were dealing with the trauma and loss in their own unique ways just as I was with my tendency to run. Towards the end of my education, I moved to Florida where my father was planning to retire and where we had another home on Sanibel Island. I attempted to survive on my own for the first time entirely and at this point was making more than my share of mistakes with career and personal life choices.

I was assigned to do two internships in hospitals in Clearwater and Sarasota, Florida. There were four students, including myself, who were completing our internships far away form Ohio in Florida. The last few months on this internship, I experienced two more losses involving two classmates who were two of the four interns from our Ohio State occupational therapy program that came to Florida.

We were all planning to go out to party with some friends we met in the hospital one night, but only two of us went out. While they were driving around a corner in a van, a motorcycle lost control and went through the roof of the van killing my one friend Hope instantly. Everyone else was ok but very shook up. At this point one of us decided to quite the program since the trauma of Hope's death affected her. We were down to only two interns now in Florida to complete our therapy degrees: Sandra and I. Then a few months after towards the end of our internship, Sandra invited me out to party with some of our new friends form the hospital. But once again I decided to stay back to study and get a good night's rest. She was living around a half hour drive from where they were partying. While on her drive home, she lost control of her brand-new car somehow and was in coma for around a month. She was never the same but did complete intensive rehab and was able to take her boards to work as an occupational therapist a few years following. We had worked together in a job after this event, but our relationship changed as she changed. I am not sure she even recalls our fun friendship in college the years prior but that was ok with me since she did live and was able to work and live a normal functional life again. I did lose two friends during that internship: one to death and one to a traumatic head

40

injury. The professors at Ohio State begged me to come back to Ohio to get out of Florida since I think they thought there was bad luck with the Florida interns. But I opted to stick it out until the end. I regret now not listening to them, but I am the kind of person that once I set my mind to start something, I usually see it to the end. Some people have described me as stubborn, but I think it is sheer determination.

I did not have any premonitions of these traumatic events with my intern friends, but my mind was on finishing school and trying to emotionally survive my previous trauma with my father and brother. So much loss, but I know I was not dealing with it only running from the losses.

During those next seven months, I did complete my college degree and remained in Florida where I found a hospital job and started my new life. While residing in Florida, I also was emerging into my new career as a medium but did not quite know where it would take me. The dreams and apparitions became more intense as were my sensitivity to other's emotions especially feeling their pain of any kind. This ability was very helpful with my work since I continued to practice as an occupational therapist with trauma and head injury with both adults and children. I was able to emotionally connect with my patients especially the ones who were in coma. I could feel their being which was not always in their body but sort of floating above their physical body. My dreams began to be more intense as they continued to give me premonitions of places and unfortunately more people in my life passing to the other side. I kept much of this information to myself and only shared the information if I trusted someone, which happened to be the people I was dreaming about, my grandmothers and mother.

We all dream but not everyone has immediate recall of the details of their dreams. As a medium and extremely sensitive person with a highly active mind, I have always had dreams that have been informative and detailed especially when I dream of my past loved ones.

A few years after the funerals of my brother and father, I began to have dreams of my father and brother. I recall two very vivid dreams of my father and deceased brother. The dreams were as real as if you recalled a fond memory in your past. The dreams' details continue in my mind as if I am looking at a photo album to this day.

In one of the dreams, my brother appeared to me with his eyeglasses. When he was physically on this earth, he had to wear glasses to see clearly from the time he was a toddler. He had multiple eye surgeries and struggled with his vision thus he relied on eyeglasses for reading and sports. In my dream, he did not have his glasses on but pointed to the glasses which were on the ground. He said to me, "I don't need these anymore. I can see without them now." I smiled and then he hugged me with an embrace I will never forget filled with warmth and comfort as I closed my eyes while more intensely feeling his presence. He then looked at me and said, "I didn't want this for you. I am sorry you have to go through this." I know he was referring to the loss and grief I had experienced. He then said, "It will all be okay in time." I closed my eyes and was crying in my dream while we continued to embrace then he disappeared while leaving his eyeglasses on the ground. I have dreamt about him periodically over the years but that first dream is very poignant in my mind.

My father on the other hand has appeared in a good number of my dreams on a frequent basis but did not talk to me only gestured the peace sign or just stared at me with a blank stare. One of my first dreams was over five years after he left us also remains very clear in my memory. In my dream, I was on a cruise ship which is odd since I had never been on a cruise and either did my father. I was walking on the ship to an ice cream parlor that was decorated in the old-fashioned way with red and white stripe décor with metal tables and chairs. My father was sitting in one of the chairs and I sat in another chair with him at the table. (I happen to consider ice cream as one of my favorite foods.) We looked at each other and he said to me, "Who am I? I looked at him and said," Don't be ridiculous you are my Dad." He smiled and that is all I recall from that dream. It reflected my father's personality and confirmation that he was communicating with words to me rather than only the peace sign seen in many previous dreams.

Dreams have always given me some message or warning, but I feel these dreams were just my brother and father checking in and letting me know they are still with me. I continue to have prophetic dreams especially prior to family members or friend's family members who will be passing usually within a few months following. I also continue to have dreams about my family on the other side especially events leading up to my mother passing and after she had passed.

A few months or so prior to my mother passing I had two dreams regarding her passing. One dream she was in the car with my stepfather. The car went into a spin and when the car came to a stop my stepfather was alone in the car. I feared my mother was going to pass in a car accident. Then a month after that dream, I dreamt I was on a train with my mother and the speed of the train was progressively accelerating. I was trying to slow down the train and felt panic with loss of control. My mother was calming sitting on the train and said to me, "You won't be able to stop this. It is supposed to happen." When I awoke, I was not sure what the train was representing in my dream but months later when my mother was diagnosed with stage IV lung cancer and only lived three weeks after being diagnosed I understood the message in the dream. She passed quickly when she was supposed to have six to twelve months more to live per the doctors' predictions. I had a dream when she was ill in the hospital prior to her going into coma that she would pass at four am and within the next few weeks. I thought maybe it was a fear dream, but it was close to the truth since she did pass at 4am and a week later. I believe the angels or maybe my family on the other side were telling me in my dream it was my mother's time and due to the fact the she went so quickly represented the fast-moving train.

I believe the dream state is a safe and easy way for God, the angels, and our loved ones to communicate with us be it a message, a warning, or a preparation premonition. When I ask to connect with my father and brother in a dream, within a few nights I always dream of them. That confirms to me they are not far from me in spirit and present.

Chapter 6- The Other Side

How do we know our past loved ones are with us? There are
times when we cannot get the loved one who passed out of our mind or

we are reminded of them through someone or an event. We cannot see them with our concrete eyes, but we sense them. It is as if our eyes are closed while we are in a room and someone comes in the room quietly while we feel that someone is near, but they do not say a word. It is the same feeling with sensing our deceased loved ones, but we cannot touch or see them. We all have this ability be it a sixth sense or some call it intuitive perception to some degree.

When I do readings, I feel the difference between a person on the earth and a person in spirit. Often before they pass, which is usually a few weeks before, I feel them in both realms but at different times during the day. Usually at night or when they are sleeping, I feel their energy or vibe as if they had passed already. It is confusing at times but interesting as if they are being presented with the opportunity to start to experience the other side.

Often, we feel the emotions of those whom we are emotionally close to be it a husband or sister even if we are miles apart. When we do talk on the phone or in person, we often hear then say something like, "I was just going to call you or I was just thinking of you and you called." How we do this is very intuitive and over the years we start to trust that these emotions and thoughts are real and not just our imagination. I have trusted my thoughts and feelings to contact someone I have a vibe on, as you may call I,t and am so grateful I did since they were needing some kind of assistance or need for support. I often tell my clients and children that you need to listen to that intuition or gut feeling, as some people call it, especially in regard to connection with our loved ones who are here or have passed.

Often when I question if my loved ones are still connecting with me, I ask for a concrete event or sign to help me believe the deceased person's presence. One example is my Notre Dame connection with my father's random sign for me.

I was born in South Bend, Indiana on, according to my mother, the hottest day in July while my father was attending Notre Dame Law School. They baptized me at the Catholic Church on the beautiful campus of Notre Dame University. My mother told me that although they both worked and shared the role of parenting me, I appeared to be calmer with my father as she recognized a strong connection I had with him even as a small child. She said even though they were poor, it was the best time in their lives as a small family. My father continued his studies at Notre Dame and completed law school. He continued to be a dedicated fan with Notre Dame football and often would go back to his alma mater.

After he passed, my family set up a scholarship in his name at Notre Dame.

There are times, I wonder if my father is still around me and I usually ask for a sign. Well, the sign consistently has been the Notre Dame logo or the appearance of something related to Notre Dame on the television. For example, I will be at a stop light and see a Notre Dame sticker on someone's car or be in line at the grocery and the guy who is in front of me will have a Notre Dame hat on. Another example is when I will turn the television on and the first show that comes on will have Notre Dame in it as in a sports event. Understand, I currently live miles away from Notre Dame in Arizona now. It is not a coincidence since it occurs 99% of the time after I ask for a sign.

Another way our passed loved ones communicate is through music. I hear that often from my clients that they coincidentally hear a sound on the radio when they are thinking of their loved one or during a special occasion like a birthday. I would hear, *Blinded By the Light* by Blue Oyster Cult during times I was thinking of my brother or near his birthday in January. This song is heard very rarely on the radio today but it is still occasionally played by oldies stations which I randomly arrive at when I am scanning for a song I like at times while in the car. About 20 years after my brother was gone, I mention to my surviving brother, Jay, if he has a song that makes him think of our brother Charlie. I never mention to this brother the song I hear that reminds me of Charlie. Weirdly, he mentioned that same song I would hear. I had never cued him before that time. That cannot be coincidence. I think Charlie had a lot to do with the selection of the song since that was a song he played on his guitar when he was physically here.

Another event with music happened less than a year after my mother passed. She always loved the song *Wind Beneath My Wings* and that was a song sung at her funeral. Her sister, my Aunt Jo and I were walking into a place where they served pizza and had a large pipe organ while she was also living in Florida close to me at the time. The moment we stepped into the restaurant, the song *Wind Beneath My Wings* was being played by the organist. We both stopped in our tracks and looked at each other in amazement while knowing that song was important to my mother. We wanted to believe my mother on the other side had something to do with the selection of the song played. My mother was close to her younger sister and the loss of my mother was very devastating for my Aunt who passed a few years after my mother with the same lung cancer diagnose. They are both on the other side now and I know they continue to send me message through dreams and music. How they do this timing of musical selections, I really do not know but I think it is an effective and heart- felt means of communication from our passed loved ones.

Birthdays are important in my family and I have been accused by others of making them an event more than most people. To me birthdays are a way of celebration of their lives. When my parents were alive, our family always had parties, nice dinners and genuinely nice gifts presented for birthdays. Now that they are gone, my party participation is limited for multiple reasons; one of them being I live far from my extended family and my children are grown. I try to not think too much about how fun and special the past was since it makes me feel down. I try to look forward but honestly, I still miss our complete family events when my mom, dad and brother were alive. One family event that stands out in my mind was one of my mother's birthdays when my father surprised my mother by having several of her friends and a Christian rock band arrive in a bus at our house when my mother was planning on going out to dinner. She was initially upset by the surprise but soon the party was rocking, and everyone seemed to have a lot of fun.

A few years ago, I had no plans for my birthday, no friends available, no husband or boyfriend and my children were with their father for the summer. I was feeling unloved and alone based on my past while missing my loved ones who enjoyed celebrating with me. I spoke to my deceased father stating that I wished he were here. I asked him for a sign that he heard me regarding my missing him and my other family members on my birthday. Twenty-four hours had passed and not a sign. No song, no random acts of kindness from a stranger, nothing to indicate that my message was delivered to the other side. A few days had gone by and I forgot about my request as I drove to the grocery store alone. While sitting at a traffic light, I saw a very colorful balloon on a string dangling on the side of the road that had written on it, "For You." It drifted directly in front of my windshield moving slowly to the across the windshield of my car then it drifted swiftly up into the sky. There was no one that I could see on the side of the road that appeared to lose a balloon. Was it coincidence? I want to believe it was my father's way of letting me know he heard me regarding my birthday request. At that moment, I did not feel as lonely and treasured the balloon memory.

This past year on my birthday unlike the previous incident written, I felt loved from my boyfriend, my family, and friends but I continue to miss my parents. I then said to my parents on the other side, if you are near me for my birthday give me a sign. I was open to what sign that would send if any. Not knowing what to expect if anything, I did not focus on this request but was hopeful as I have been in the past. A few days later, I was walking the dog and saw one red rose across the street from my house on the street. I picked it up and brought it home believing that this was my sign since my father then my mother gave me one red rose on my birthday when they were here. Coincidence or not? I want to believe this was not just coincidence but my sign. How often does anyone see one red rose randomly placed in a residential neighborhood next to the curb and across from your home.

Often, I tell my clients who would like a sign from their deceased loved one to ask and believe your request will be granted. I have heard many times during readings, they want to hear a very specific sign or phrase. Sometimes if that specific sign does not show up during the reading then they question why or the validity of the reading. My answer is the person on the other side does not choose to connect with this sign. My advice is to be open for whatever comes through during the reading and if the deceased person chooses, they will reveal a validation of some kind either during the reading or soon after. I did a reading for someone recently who said they were not sure her father was around she and her family. She said she felt his presence very strong after he passed but now, she felt he was gone. During the reading, he came through and brought up something about new carpet. She teared up and said we just moved into her house and put in new carpet yesterday. To me this was a message that her father was still visiting them even though my client did not feel it nor did she hear a preconceived specific item or song as a sign.

Another sign I see often is finding coins as a message from a loved one. I call them Pennies from Heaven. A few years ago, I was working at a hospital in Phoenix. I worked long and very physically exhausting hours with my focus on my patients and not myself. I had a dream that my mother was dropping dimes in one of the hallways of the hospital. My mother was a nurse and felt comfortable in the hospital setting. It was a very cool dream in that I saw my mother again, but she was giving me dimes; lots of dimes. I woke up from the dream thinking maybe I am going to win the lottery, or someone was going to gift me a lot of dimes. A few days after the dream I had forgotten about the dimes and was going about my business at work when I was going down the hallway that was in my dream and looked on the floor. There were about thirty or more dimes scattered on the hallway carpet, just like my dream. That was a sign that my mother was with me. I am sure she was visiting me at work especially when I worked with critically ill patients. In case you wondered, yes, I did pick up the dimes and placed them in my pocket.

Another personal coin incident occurred recently when I asked my father to let me know he was guiding my children and me. I, like some of my clients, was not feeling like my father was near me. I like to walk early in the morning to clear my mind and pray while also getting some exercise. I was rapidly walking down the street with the birds singing and the sun barely rising above the home in my neighborhood. I had mentally tracked out my route this morning but as an afterthought I quickly turned the corner and changed my preset route. Three feet into the new walking route, I looked on the asphalt street and saw again thirty pennies. I again picked them up and said Thank You Dad to myself. Many times, prior to that incident over the years, I have asked my father to give me a sign he hears me when I asked him if he is around or helping me. The Notre Dame sign occurs often but also within a few days after my request I will find pennies in a parking lot, in a public bathroom or once in a purse I purchased. Some would say it is coincidence, but my pennies have appeared along with the Notre Dame sign 99% of the time if I ask for confirmation. Some would say I am just looking for a sign but no I am busy going about my day and forget that I have asked for a sign. It is not as if I ask for the sign then ...poof I get my answer immediately. But it is no longer then a few days after my request. The Pennies from Heaven are often familiar signs other clients and mediums have shared with me as proof that our loved ones are hearing us on the other side. How they plant these coins, is a mystery to me but I do appreciate it and often ask "How do you do this?" But the answer never comes. So, I am happy for the affirmation despite its mystery method of penny placement.

Chapter 7- Reading for Others

Growing up I always knew I was intuitive with family and friend's matters based on my dreams and intuitive feelings. I was very intuitive prior to someone in the family who would pass soon. I also knew that I had sort of an empathic connection with loved ones both here and on the other side. An example of this precognitive intuition was with my paternal grandmother growing up. As I became busy with high school and college activities, I was not visiting grandmother as often as I did when I was younger, but our strong connection never lost its strength. I would be thinking about calling her on the phone and within the hour, she would call me. This happened often. Grandmother has been on the other side for more than 20 years and I continue to feel her presence and hear her in my dreams.

Doing formal readings for those outside on my family and friend circle was not something I pursued until my late twenties when a friend asked me to try a reading with her. She invited me to her home one evening with wine and Hors Oeuvres, which I thought was very fancy for an amateur medium, but I appreciated the generosity. We sat in her living room on the floor and I silenced my thoughts and proceeded to feel, visualize in my mind's eye and hear messages from people in her past who had passed on. One of her family members I vividly recall was her uncle who committed suicide. He did not tell me those facts but showed me a rope on his neck and was telling me repeatedly, "I am sorry." She had not told me about her family background thus I initially thought I was picking up on someone that may have lived in her house prior. She was speechless and told me when she was composing herself from crying, that the man I was describing was her uncle who hung himself. When the reading was done, she told me she had never told anyone of her friends about her uncle. She said the reading gave her peace and resolution. I was amazed myself how information from the other side was communicated to me so clearly and easily. At that moment, I decided I would continue to provide to others comfort and answer questions about their loved ones who had passed through medium readings.

Personally, I knew that having a medium reading was more therapeutic than going to counseling for my grief concerns with the loss of my brother and father. The medium reading answered many ambiguities and helped me realize that a connection of love with someone lives on even when they pass. I continued to do readings for random family members and trusted friends who were open to having a medium reading but started my journey as a professional reaching out to those outside of my circle. The difficulty I felt though with this journey was how do I deal with the social stigmas and bias most people had about psychic mediums, especially my Catholic family.

My family 's beliefs were Catholic based but on my mother's side of the family there is a native American heritage with beliefs of dream messages, listening to your intuition and paying attention to signs in nature. My father's side of the family did not have those beliefs thus I was felt more comfortable talking to my mother's side of the family with more acceptance regarding medium work. Also, my mother had an interest in astrology and reading tarot cards but like my other family members, was very devoted to our Catholic faith and practices which did not reinforce in our education medium work. I knew many family members then and to this day have prejudices regarding psychics and mediums. The message communicated to me was psychics are not real, most do not help you and psychics are from the devil. These beliefs from my past affected my decision to restrict being open with my abilities and newly chosen vocation with most people even today. I struggled with this for years and many times asked myself, "Am I willing to change how people view me and risk being rejected by many? Am I willing to be judged and criticized by society's bias's and misunderstanding about what mediums do and the benefits of how they help others with grief work?" I went through a period over a year about 10 years ago, when I doubted my abilities even though I continued to have dreams, see ghost like figures, and sense that someone or someplace would be a part of my future. People from my past whom I did readings for continued to call me for another reading which motivated me to continue my medium work and commitment to help others.

The word got out that Eliza could connect to passed loved ones and my client base was no longer friends but complete strangers who wanted readings. So here is when my medium work took a turn. I did not and still do not think of my medium work as a job or a career but something I passionately believe in that assists those in need to have some peace and realization that their loved ones are still with them even when they pass.

Now I had a secret that I choose to not reveal to some family members, co-workers, and some friends. So, the question was how long would I be able to keep this a secret?

Chapter 8 –Running from Grief

It had been six years since I started college and since the accident occurred. I was living in Florida after finishing internships in Florida hospitals. I had new friends, a new sports car, and my first job out of college. My father had plans to move to Florida and retire when he was of retirement age. He loved to sail, fish, water ski, and snorkel thus Florida living suited all his hobbies. My father and grandmother had purchased a condominium on the beach in Sanibel, Florida where we would visit often during the year. But since he had traveled to the other side, we only went to our second home a few times then my mother decided to sell the property. I never understood why she did this. She sold the home in

Akron, my father's sports cars, his two boats, and the Florida condominium. I guess she figured it would help us with our grief if all the property reminders of our past were wiped out and a clean slate was to be created. But my reaction was quite the contrary and I missed all those reminders when they were gone. So, I decided to move to Florida since the emotional pain of staying in Ohio without them was excruciating and any physical semblance of them was also gone which would have given me some comfort. My mother and brother were dealing with their own grief in remotely different manners and I felt the need to do my own thing in Florida.

My move to Florida with a new sports car while living near the beach was my way of fulfilling my dear father's dream to retire there. My living family, which was my mother and brother, did not seem to understand my reasoning for moving to Florida but I strongly felt the need to do so. I knew no one in Sarasota but proceeded to start my own new life in a fresh way while continuing to heal on my own.

My first job in Florida as an occupational therapist was at a local hospital where I met a physician whom I started dating. I had attained one of my goals of completing six years of college and now my next goal was to find someone who I could live with forever. My emotional status was very vulnerable and fragile, and my judgement of character was flawed most likely from my dealing with the grief of my father and brother. At the time, I thought I was fine while partying with this doctor and his friends who were unlike any other group I had ever associated with before. I grew up with upper to upper middle-class friends with Christian and Jewish backgrounds, but this boyfriend was a practicing Muslim and he was raised in India. I was learning about the delicious Indian food, the practices of the Muslim religion, and his Indian culture. There were times when we would get together with a large majority of his friends and colleagues and I was the only white and non-Muslim person there. I did not speak their language but made due since most his friends also spoke English. I also learned how to deal with infidelity and abuse in relationships while denying that my boyfriend had serious problems with women. I thought at the time that he did not mean to hurt me he just had a substance abuse problem. These ways of life where very foreign to my cultural, family, and moral backgrounds thus my coping skills were not developed for dealing with this type of problem. Also, my self-esteem began to disintegrate the more I engaged in this relationship. This became my first and only codependent relationship. It was very weird for me overall but possibly for some reason I persisted to stay in this unhealthy relationship.

After the verbal and emotional abuse came the physical abuse which would come out of nowhere after two years of dating. When my jaw and fingers where fractured from him beating me up, I decided to get some professional help but did not tell my family who was many miles away in Ohio. The counselors asked why I did not turn this abusive physician in and my reply was one of fear since he told me if I ever told anyone he did this to me he would admit me to a hospital and say I was psychotic. He had a good standing in the community and was exceedingly popular with the girls he worked with as I found out later. He would tell these girls that I was only the woman that decorated his house as I heard one night while catching him in bed with someone else. He was much older than I and soon realized I was running away from anything remotely familiar to my prior life in Ohio when my brother and father were alive. I felt that this older doctor of 15 years my senior became somewhat of a father figure to me but I did not see that until many years later when I became more emotionally healthy. My father never abused anyone and never even raised his voice to me. I realized I was still maladaptively grieving and my way of coping was to engage in this crazy relationship.

My relationship with this physician became very toxic both for he and I as I found out later through counseling and having some professional contact with him at one of my jobs.

My paternal grandmother was still alive at the time. She was very intuitively close to me, as mentioned prior, all my life and she somehow figured out I was in trouble living in Florida. I visited her while spending some time in Ohio on a vacation and she said to me that I should "Run not walk away," from this relationship. I knew from her comment and stern demeanor that she was serious. After this conversation with her, I broke off the relationship without any doubt or fear while receiving psychotherapy and then finding a new job far away from this physician who to this day just added to my unwillingness to be emotionally vulnerable with anyone. It has gotten easier with emotional support from professionals and friends through the years, but I am not the same person I was before the tragic brother and father accident and this abusive relationship. I have learned to survive and appreciate living for today.

I will say the loss of my father, brother, grandmothers, and my mother has forced me to continue to work on my coping skills with grieving. I continue at times to overreact and have mini-panic attacks when not hearing from a loved one over a short period such as 10 hours or when they go out of town. The emotional bruises and brokenness have never entirely gone away but I have learned to cope. My religious faith and use of meditation have help me on a personal level to wake up each day and appreciate all the gifts that most of us take for granted. Every day is a gift and an opportunity.

My compassion for those who have dealt with an abusive relationship and grieving is more empathetic then someone that has never gone through those types of traumas in their lives. I guess I never let it break me, but it made me stronger and more willing to continue my mediumship and therapy work to reach out to others who have had similar experiences.

Chapter 9- Marriage and Children

Emerging into my thirties was my biological clock. Since I was a young girl, I wanted to be a mother. In fact, I wanted five children with a supportive loving husband to partner with me. As I turned thirty years old, I did not have a prospective male in my life who could be my husband. My mother told me to start looking for pans and china since I may not ever get married to receive these items in the traditional manner, which was during the engagement period. Well I took half of my mother's advice and did buy new pans but the china I was hopeful that someone would come around in the next few years to marry me.

That is what happened one year later when I was thirty-one. I met my husband through a friend who was getting married. She wanted music with duets at her wedding and found out I sang at weddings. I did not have anyone I could do the duet with, so she managed to find the other half of the duet which was a man with a naturally beautiful voice.

When I first met him, we were walking into the church to practice the songs we were going to sing at my friend's wedding. The sunlight was shining in his crystal blue eyes and I lost my breath for a few seconds since at the moment I just knew this was going to be my future husband. Five months later we got married and sang to each other with the same song we sang at my friend's wedding when we first met. It was a very romantic first five months then it turned into a downward swirl of depression and mixed emotions on my end. I loved the fact that I was married but realized that this marriage would not last a lifetime. I gave it my 200% but then after two children and many arguments filed for divorce. Now I believe, he was only to pass into my life to be the father of my loving girls and that was it. It was a difficult divorce, but I knew I would be fine raising my children with little help from my husband depending on his emotional status which was up and down with depression.

Twenty-one years later, I am still single, but I have my two now adult children who fill my life with happiness, fun and sometimes craziness. I am blessed to have them in my life and realize, God did not intend for me to be a married when I was raising them. I have had past opportunities to get married with two other partners, but it did not work out in the direction. I was with a partner to a beautiful man who I also knew when I first met him would be in my life. He had been in my life over a decade which is longer than any other relationship I have had in my lifetime. But now I am on my own and he is also a person of my past. He reminded me of both my father and brother in many ways, but it was time for me to move on this past year. I feel the traumas of my past losses of family and the divorce have contributed to my not getting close again to the place of marriage. I believe it has taken me over forty years to heal to the point of having a healthy committed relationship now.

My children have been my priority since they were born, and they continue to be to this day. I always made sure they had a good education and spiritual connection as I raised them Catholic. They also grew up hearing about my medium experiences along with other family members who had similar abilities.

We lived in Florida from the time they were born until 2005 when I fought my way out of Florida to sunny Arizona where they continued their education to this day. They were both in college and starting to pursue their own dreams as I now write the story of my life which is one of my lifelong dreams; to tell my story.

Often people have asked me if my children have similar psychic abilities as I and I answer, "Yes, they do." Both my children have abilities with precognition regarding others especially us as a family. One of my children can see and feel the presence of spirit on the other side but she is afraid which discourages her to be of assistance to others. My other daughter has more empathic abilities with others and with an environment. She also chooses to not further her psychic skills. But both are very verbal with me with what they feel and if they sense something is off or going on. Remember, I did not do anything professional with my abilities until I was nearly thirty years old but did communicate to chosen and trusted family members when I had a dream, a vision, fear, and precognitive prediction. I feel it is a personal choice to work with spirit for the betterment of others who are dealing with grief and personal conflicts. It is a calling and a choice if one desires to use their medium psychic abilities and not a something to be forced.

With both my children having abilities, I have emphasized to them to work with prayer and listen to that inner voice. Growing up psychic, I realized how challenging and difficult it was to have these abilities without guidance and social acceptance. I always felt I had to hide my abilities since that was communicated to me as a child. As a result, I developed my program, Intuitive Tools for Kids with the goal to help sensitive children and their parents to help the children and their parents first to understand what it feels like to have psychic abilities, and second to manage these abilities in an emotionally positive manner.

I have lectured throughout the country about the Intuitive Tools for Kids program since its development with parents verbalizing appreciation and a greater understanding of their psychic children. The key most important message I have given to these parents is to listen; just listen without judgement and with loving acceptance. The children on the other hand seem to be drawn to me while wanting to just to be in my presence as if you have connected with familiar culture or family member. I believe that these children can learn protection techniques including meditation as early as four years old. I also believe all children are born into this earthly realm with intuitive abilities of varying degrees. But the world does not always reinforce the practice of intuition currently, so their abilities become either dormant or just not needed in their life. Some cultures more than others presently encourage the development of spiritual and psychic abilities while some cultures instill fear and misconceptions of the abilities. My hope is that in time, all cultures will have more acceptance and understanding of one's psychic abilities and not shy away from them due to fears or misunderstanding.

Chapter 10 – Certifications

My medium readings work was beginning to pick up with word of mouth and my one afternoon a week appearance at a store in town that offered readings to the public. But I felt like there was more I needed to do to further my career. I saw the television show *Medium* and then looked up the show's medium's name since the show was based on real people. I found that she was affiliated with an organization in Tucson, Arizona that studied mediums and that they were interviewing and looking for mediums to assist with research. There was no doubt in my mind that I wanted to be one of the research mediums and

coincidentally I had just moved to Scottsdale, Arizona which was a short

drive from Tucson. I recalled calling Dr. Julie Beischel of Windbridge

Institute who was conducting the interviews and assessments of

prospective mediums. She provided me with very extensive and detailed

information on the testing processing and work that needed to be done

prior to certification as a research medium with the Institute. Following a

couple of years of completing the very intensive work of personality tests,

studying books on grief work, and medium testing, I was uncertain on the

results and questioned if I would be considered. Some of the testing was

performed without a person on the other end of the phone but the

person was aware I was connecting with their loved one during a test

reading. Some readings there was a person on the phone but they were

not responding to the information coming in from the medium and a few

readings with the sitter I was reading was able to provide some feedback

to the medium. Despite my doubts, I was one of the chosen mediums to

participate in research with the Windbridge Institute. Currently, I am now

a certified level 5 research medium and am very thankful to Dr. Julie

Beischel for the opportunity to be a part of the amazing and ground

breaking scientific research that continues to grow with the extensive efforts and brilliance in studying life after death and communication with the deceased created and conducted by Windbridge Institute. For more information about Windbridge Institute follow the link: www.windbridge.org

Another affiliated organization was also offering the opportunity to be a certified medium. This organization was the Forever Family Foundation with Phran and Bob Ginsberg who founded the organization to assist others who have experienced grief and loss of a loved one. I then became certified with this foundation and again am extremely grateful for the opportunity to assist with the goals of the foundation. I have participated in their weekend seminars and internet radio appearances while speaking of my programs and conducting readings for those in need. For more information on Forever Family Foundation follow this link: www.foreverfamilyfoundation.org

Both amazing organizations have assisted me as well as many others to understand more about the afterlife process and the progression of grief work available. They also have helped my career by posting my website and information which has provided me with clients who trust that the certified mediums listed are reputable. I am proud to be a part of both organizations and would highly recommend anyone interested to read both their websites, and follow the current research, affiliated books, and future volunteer opportunities.

I have often said that we are in the pioneer stages of truly understanding what happens after we die and how we connected with those who have passed. There is much more to learn and understand on a scientific basis which I believe will contribute to ridding of the social biases of mediums and psychics.

When I tell most people that I am a medium their entire demeanor immediately changes. They become intrigued but suspicious. I had a coworker at one of my occupational therapy jobs tell me that she cannot talk to or interact with me because she was afraid, I was always reading her mind. This is so far from the truth since I am in a more relaxed state with focused intention of doing a reading and empathically connecting with someone's mood and sometimes thoughts. Granted I do see and hear things randomly or feel an energy either positive or negative around others when I am not in this focused state but it is not on an hourly basis but definitely on a daily basis. I believe many of my close friends and family members are moderately accepting of my medium work but since I have not read for them and will not do so. Only the family members who have similar abilities understand to varying degree what it feels like to have medium abilities. Thus, I do not freely reveal to people what I do as my second career as a medium. There continues to be a lot of misconceptions and suspicions. The passion to help those who have experienced loss as I have and to help them understand their loved ones are still around them with the love they had for them while they were on this earth continues and strengthens after they have passed. This passion continues to drive me forward with my role as a medium and it does not matter if my friends and family do not 100% understand. I know those who are grieving or have unanswered questions about their loved ones who have passed are benefiting from the readings I do and that is enough for me to continue this work despite the biases and misunderstandings.

Even my own children doubt and question my abilities since I told them I will not read for them but honestly, I am more intuitively connected to both as my parents and siblings were to me. I am sure they often think that they would want a mother who is not intuitively aware especially when they are doing something that would not be in their best interest. I think most parents are aware when their children are up to something but my poor kids have it doubled with the amount of intuitive connection especially if they are trying to pull the wool over my eyes as one would say. I remember my father used to tell me he always knew I was lying, which wasn't very often, because my nose would turn red but I believe he was just intuitively connected to me as I feel he continues to be even though he has been on the other side since 1977.

My children have often said that they are somewhat embarrassed to tell their friends that their mom is a medium. I have asked them to be careful who they discuss this with since the biases and misconceptions continue in society but thankfully are diminishing due to the efforts of the Windbridge Institute and Forever Family Foundation which continue to educate and inform others of their missions and extensive research efforts. My hope is that my grandchildren, which I currently do not have yet, will live in a society where being a medium will be accepted and respected as any other helping and healing profession. I hope my involvement in these organizations also contributes to the future of understanding mediums and the afterlife.

Chapter 11-Writings and Inspirations

While residing in Florida, I was working on my first published

book, Daysee The Delinquent Angel. When I started writing it, I did not

have a title but was clear on the story line about a young angel in training

coming to earth while helping special education children. I based the

story on children I had worked with in the school as an occupational therapist and my vision that they all had a special angel that guided them but this one was very empathetic and inexperienced. I also incorporated people in my life who had passed who were angels into the story line. But I needed a title and I wanted the title to blend with my Intuitive Tools for Kids program that was in the development stages. One night in the middle of the night, I was starting to awaken to check on my children and I saw a vision of a pink winged angel with a cherub face with blonde hair and blue eyes and I saw very clearly the word Daysee which I interpreted as the name of the angel in the book as well as the intended title. I wrote it down so I would not forget and from that day forward, Daysee was created. I had moved to Arizona a few years after that vision and then formally completed the book while self-publishing Daysee The Delinquent Angel. Since then I have completed the sequel titled Last Wishes which is the continuation of Daysee's journey on earth with the same children as in the first book but with an added angel who has the characteristics as my brother who had passed when he was fifteen years old.

I had always written poems, and stories since I was a child thus creating these two books was a lifelong goal of mine to write a story that inspires but entertains. My other lifelong goal is to write this book and tell my story in hopes again to inspire and help others understand what it is like to grow up as a medium. I continue to become lost in process of time and space when I am writing where hours go by and it feels like minutes to me. When I used to paint and compose music, I experienced the same elimination of the concept of time. I often compare this process to what I believe is the concept of time on the other side which I believe is quite different to our earthly conception.

Often during a reading when a person has passed unexpectantly, like in a car accident, they communicate to me that they did not realize they had passed for a while until someone comes to them from the other side and tells them they have been deceased for years but they felt like it was days. I can imagine it will be a learning process to shift your soul's understanding of time, place, and communication. But for those who engage in a creative lost in time project, I believe this transition is not as challenging.

Another inspiration came when I was trying to come up with a name for my company. I wanted a name that communicated to others that we all are inspired to change and to listen to our intuition instead of only going about our routine day while only thinking our way through life. Over a course of months, nothing came to mind until I was visiting some of my dear friends in Gig Harbor, Washington. We had our elementary school children with us at lunch at a restaurant on the harbor. I was uninterested in any of the conversations between my friends and the children, thus became lost in looking at the water and the beautiful array of yachts and boats at the harbor. Not sure of what sparked my initial thought, but I heard a name in my mind of *Intuitive Inspirations.* Like the dream I had a Daysee this came in like a flash in my mind's eye but this time I was awake although relaxed in my feelings. I wrote the name down on a napkin and told my friends the name I liked for my company and they liked it too.

Thus, the company Intuitive Inspirations LLC was formed which now offers consultations, medium and psychic readings, meditation education, speaking topics and selling of my books and writings.

Inspiration can come at any time in our lives and can be a catalyst for change. I believe our guides, angels and God are connecting with us to move forward with our changes. The secret is to intuitively listen and then let it grow to flower. Sometimes, it is appearing to be an impossible vision, but I know we all can create what seems impossible today something possible and fulfilling for our future.

When I was in my twenties, I asked a wise gentleman who I am sorry to say I do not recall his name, what am I supposed to do with my ability to do readings and write. I told him I love to do these things, but I do not know the purpose of them in my life. He so wisely said to me, "Just Share Your Gifts." It seems very simple but at the time I couldn't figure out how but the inspiration and doors opened to me as I kept my vision and goal in check as I write this book and do many readings. My advice to you is to not doubt or stop that thought or what seems like a crazy idea but take one step forward towards your idea and as my mother would say, if it is meant to be it will be. Again, it will easily flow without effort and it will be simple if we just share it with those here on earth and those on the other side. We are the change so be the change for yourself and others to benefit from.

Chapter 12- **Your Reading**

Many people have asked what do I do to prepare for my reading? Over the years of doing readings, I have been asked this question. My best advice to someone who has never had a medium reading is trust the information is what you deceased loved one chooses to communicate and most importantly to relax. There was a woman who came to me twenty years ago for an in person reading who was extremely nervous. She had not had a reading before the reading with me and was referred from a friend. I recall she had a journal book in preparation to write the information down from the reading which she placed on my dining table while seated to the left of me. Why I remember her so distinctly from the many people I read for is because her hands were nervously shaking, and her voice was trembling. Before we got started, I asked her if she was ok and wanted to proceed. She said yes since she had many questions about her life and her loved ones. I explained to her that it would benefit both of us if she could take a few deep breaths and calm herself, otherwise my ability to read her may be more challenging. I then proceeded to tell her more about my past and why I became a medium. After hearing that information, she calmed down a bit and the hand shaking stopped. The other reason I recall this woman was I was able to connect for the first time with spiritual circle of others on the other side who assist me with doing body scans to provide helpful information for the person's physical and emotional wellbeing. I sense and see "hot spots" on someone from a past or current injury or illness. Then I hear or seen recommendations from this spiritual circle. This woman's toddler son was having seizures and I saw him being tested for seizures, but the physicians were unable to do anything to stop the seizures completely. I then was smelling and tasting chlorine and asked her if they had a swimming pool with chlorine? She replied "Yes, they do." The advice I heard was the chlorine was somehow adversely affecting her son's health. Months later, she contacted me again and told me they removed the chlorinated water and replaced it with salt. She also told me within a few days following the removal of the chlorine, her son's seizure activity had stopped, and he was no longer on any medication. I believe when I connected with this circle twenty years ago, I sensed only about ten spiritual beings came through to provide information. Currently, when I perform a body scan, I sense there are close to one hundred or more spiritual beings that connect with me as they appear in a large circle. I am not sure who they are but know that have provided helpful information to others during my readings. I am very appreciative for their assistance since many people are searching for alternative methods for healing both their physical body and their emotions. As I believe there is a strong connection with both. I always emphasize the information is not medical advice since I am not a physician but information that comes through is for them to decide what they choose to do with it; be it listen to it, follow it or ignore it. It is their choice.

The other advice I have for those who have a reading is to not test the medium. If you are having a reading to see if we are legitimate, then the skepticism affects the ease in connecting with those who have passed. It is not that I cannot connect, it somehow puts a tension on the reading which increases my anxiety thus not allowing me to connect on a psychic level as easily. Sometimes, those who have passed want the skeptic to have a reading, since I believe it is never a mistake that someone is coming for a reading so I proceed in knowing there is a reason for the reading. I find there are less and less skeptics over the past few years since social acceptance and interest with mediums has improved. Also, due to the fact, I have been already tested with Windbridge Institute assures others that my reading is more legitimate. Again, I am thankful for organizations like the Windbridge Institute that support us.

The last word of advice I often tell others is that the information your loves one is choosing to share with you if up to them. Often people want to know if their loved one felt pain prior to dying or if they knew they were in the room. That information is usually shared before the person even asks me the question. I have had a few readings over the years, where people have a specific item or word they want to hear that they have asked their loved one on the other side to communicate to confirm that they are really coming through. Most of the time a mention of this request is honored but when it is not then the person questions the entire reading. I often advice others to be open to whatever information their loved one wants to tell us during the reading. More often than not, the person who has past comes through as if they are either in their late twenties or early thirties since I believe that is for most of us the prime of our lives both mentally and physically. I recently did a reading for a woman whose mother passed from cancer and had lost all her hair. The mother came through with blonde beautiful hair then showed me a scarf that she would wear that was more fashionable in the 1950's. The woman said her mother always protected her hair when she was outside with scarfs and prided herself on having a nice hairdo. She stated that she wanted to be remembered looking like that with hair and her scarf rather than the bald woman that others saw prior to her passing.

A few weeks after my mother had passed from lung cancer and a stroke, I dreamt about her. Near the last days of her life, she became bedridden and was in sort of a comatose state. Her 64-year-old body was debilitating as she was cared for in Hospice for those final five days. The vision I have of her lying there with her physical body breaking down was very difficult for me to share or relive as I write this. She was a very physically attractive woman and had a very lively spirt with laughter and love for everyone she met. In my dream, she was in the ICU of the hospital she went to prior to Hospice House and she asked me, "Honey, what happened to me?" I was in the dream and said to her "Mom, you died." She looked beautiful with her salon perfect blonde hair and was thin. She looked like when I was a child in her thirties as she smiled at me and said, "Oh, Good." She did not want to get old as she told me how she hated her wrinkles many times as she was getting older. I know she wanted to be joined again with my father and brother whom she missed everyday after they went to the other side. She looked happy and healthy. I try to keep this beautiful image of my mother when I think of her.

When you think of your passed loved ones, think of them as happy and healthy. That is how most people want to be recalled from my experiences during most of my readings. They sometimes refer to photos that are displayed in the sitter's homes.

Sometimes, when a past loved one did something harmful or hurtful prior to their passing, for instance if they were physically abusive or had a severe drug problem, I seen them behind a dark black curtain and they timidly peek from behind the curtain. They often ask if the sitter desires to hear from them and often ask for some form of forgiveness. It is up to the sitter if they want to connect with this person. Forgiveness is something we all struggle with at times. I feel when we forgive ourselves or others, we free them and us with peace between others thus allowing us to grow and not survive in a negative state of mind. It really does not serve us in the long run. I do not know about you, but animosity, negativity, and bitterness are not emotions that I want to carry around with me. I am not saying to forget but to forgive to heal ourselves. Many times, those who ask for forgiveness on the other side communicate to me that they have some form of penance or work they have been assigned to do to help others who are still on earth. Some may call it karma. I often say prayers for that soul who may be a lost soul. I ask the sitter if they feel inclined to pray for the person who is on the other side asking for forgiveness too. I can tell you not many people are inclined to not forgive depending on relationship and severity of what happened prior to the person passing they are connecting with.

Chapter 13-Your Connection to the Other Side

One memorable reading of a family wanting to connect with their deceased mother helped me to understand that most people coming for readings do not know how to communicate with their deceased loved ones. We were sitting at my dining room table, as their mother was communicating the confirmation that the information, they were hearing from me was actually their mother and grandmother. Tears were rolling down most of their cheeks as I described what she was feeling at the time of her death and how she is doing now on the other side. They asked me questions as to where their mother wanted her ashes buried and any specific requests regarding her last wishes. Their mother was in coma the last week of her life here on earth and there was a lot of unanswered questions. Two of the family members then proceeded to yell very loudly that they missed and loved their mother as they looked up to the ceiling as if their mother was on my roof or floating in the corners of my 30 ft. ceiling. That is when I realized that most people don't realize their loved ones are standing right next to them and they hear them, feel their emotions and are able to touch them but most of us are not sure of the connection since we are unable to see them like we did when they were on the earth. I proceeded to explain to the family as I calmed them down from crying that their mother was here with us standing next to them as she went from person to person hugging them.

Often during a reading, I also explained they can hear us and are aware of what is going on in our lives now. They do not leave us since the bonds of love intertwine us together forever. Most people just want to know if their departed loved one is okay on the other side.

During most medium readings, people say to me I feel my father, mother or husband who has departed near me. Some say I talk to him in the car since I think he is there. Some explain how a certain song will come on the radio randomly that was their brother's favorite song. Some say they feel their husband or wife with them at night when they are going to sleep. Many people have said they hear them call out their name at random times. I have had people come for a reading wanting to connect with their departed mother or father then the departed communicate to me what other family members are doing at that time especially if it is spouse are doing. They often tell me that they are hearing the living spouse talk to them as of the departed were still alive. The departed often tell me that they connect with the young children in the family. The sitter often tells me that usually the young children tell them that they say Papa or the man near my bed at night is your brother who died. They also very often tell me that the children are never fearful of this connection. Thus, they come to a medium for clarity since all these situations are not concrete situations that they cannot clearly explain with the other five senses.

During a typical reading, I usually feel like I and the deceased loved one are being tested. The person receiving the reading waits to hear from someone that they may have had a relationship with; be it a grandparent, parent, spouse, or good friend. Then I usually describe something about their physical appearance or personality which usually but not always relaxes the person receiving the reading. Then the deceased show me in my mind's eye a place, or sometimes an object that represents them such as their favorite chair or a piece of jewelry. Most of the time the image makes sense but sometimes it does not at that time, but I write the information down anyways. Often, I receive after the fact communication from the sitter who had a reading that they figured out later what this all meant. The information often is a confirmation when someone has had a dream or a vision of the same object.

Most people just want to know their deceased loved one is near them or is aware of what is going on in their lives. I had a reading where the grandfather came through with bells ringing in the background of the phone but neither one of us had bells near us. The person stated that they believe that this was confirmation that their grandfather was coming through clearly. The person said they had heard these bells at other times since their grandfather had passed.

One of my frequent clients, mentions that their three-year-old son sees Papa all the time in his room when he is playing alone. The client has never doubted her son but just needed confirmation that the Papa is the one visiting her son. She stated she just knows that Papa is around her family since she feels his presence quite often.

When we want to connect with our decease loved ones but do not feel it, I often recommend asking them to show us a familiar sign. One of my best friend's mother comes through with hummingbirds which is such a beautiful sign. Another friend says she sees frogs since her mother loved frogs. Another friend sees butterflies that stay around them for a longer time than usual. My friends tell me the sign is all they need to confirm their loved ones are close to them and hear them.

Our deceased loved ones tell me during readings that they want to connect with us and they love us. They connect through dreams, signs, visions and interfering with items that are electrically charged such as flashing lights and radios. Sometimes, they tell me that they are trying to get through to their loved one but the loved one is not paying attention or is blocking the communication due to extreme grief or anger.

The most common inquiry I have is people want to know if their deceased loved one is okay. Are they not in pain anymore or are not alone? I have never heard or felt that someone on the other side is in some sort of physical pain and most of them are feeling peace overall. If their passing was traumatic or self-induced from for instance suicide, I can feel some mixed feelings from the deceased but other than that they are not in pain. Sometimes, I hear that they were not ready to die yet or they needed more time to do things they wanted to do. They tell me they see their loved ones crying or arguing with other regarding their loss. Most of the time, they are assisting to assist with this grief or the process of reducing the arguing.

One of the courses I have taught is the Art and Beauty of Journaling to Connect with those who have passed. The first time I taught this course, I provided the class with a journaling book and explained how to connect in a quite simple and relaxed manner. But the most important notion I stressed in the course is to ask the loved one you want to connect with to communicate and believe that what you are writing is from this deceased person. I have done this practice personally to connect with my father and mother many times. I have saved the papers in my journal and then went back after many years and read what I wrote as messages from my father. I am always amazed at how relevant the information is to my life and my family's life but when I was writing the information much of what I was writing did not make any sense at the time.

I do want to emphasize that one must have faith and trust that our loved ones are near us and not floating around in some cloud in the sky. We need to understand that their love never disappears or diminishes. My father has said to me during one dream when I asked where have you been? "There's a man standing next to you," in a very funny and dry sense of humor that he was known for. I titled this book on this phrase to emphasize our loved ones are close to us more than we are conscious of. I want to believe this is true since I feel his love and strength near me often. I never doubted my father when he was alive and I continue to not doubt any connection or message I hear from him or any other of my loved ones who have passed to a place of perfect peace.

Acknowledgments and Thank You

Many thanks go to all the wonderful people who have supported me in this journey to not fear but forge ahead with my beliefs and helpful pursuits for others. Amongst those who have supported me on this journey are first my family members, especially my mother and some of my dear friends. I also am grateful for all those whose dreams to expand the horizon for learning more about what happens when we are deceased and how we continue to pursue connection with those who have passed. I especially want to thank the Windbridge Institute for Applied Science and the Forever Family Foundation. They have assisted me to improve my confidence and credibility from the certification process they offered and the exposure to my clients. They also have provided international contact for those who are requesting more of a connection with their passed loved ones. I honestly believe without the support and encouragement from those I have performed readings for during the years, I would not be continuing my readings. They have continued to enrich my spirit with their hope and confidence in reaching out to those who have passed and each other.

Eliza Rey

Contact Eliza through her website at www.elizarey.com for more information.

www.ingramcontent.com/pod-product-compliance
Ingram Content Group UK Ltd.
Pitfield, Milton Keynes, MK11 3LW, UK
UKHW021422280425
5663UKWH00038B/1106